NOW, THAT'S BIG!

Published by Creative Education
P.O. Box 227, Mankato, Minnesota 56002
Creative Education is an imprint of The Creative Company
www.thecreativecompany.us

Design and Production by The Design Lab
Printed in the United States of America

Photographs by 123RF (Gary718), Alamy (Mary Evans Picture Library, Chuck
Pefley), BigStockPhoto, Corbis (Bettmann, Underwood & Underwood),
Dreamstime (Avlitrato), Getty Images (Lorentz Gullachsen), iStockphoto
(Joshua Haviv)

Library of Congress Cataloging-in-Publication Data
Riggs, Kate.
Empire State Building / by Kate Riggs.
p. cm. — (Now that's big!)
Includes index.
ISBN 978-1-58341-703-4
1. Empire State Building (New York, N.Y.)—Juvenile literature.
2. New York (N.Y.)—Buildings, structures, etc.—Juvenile literature. I. Title.
F128.8.E46R54 2009   974.7'1—dc22   2007052339

First edition

9 8 7 6 5 4 3 2 1

TE BUILDING

BY KATE RIGGS

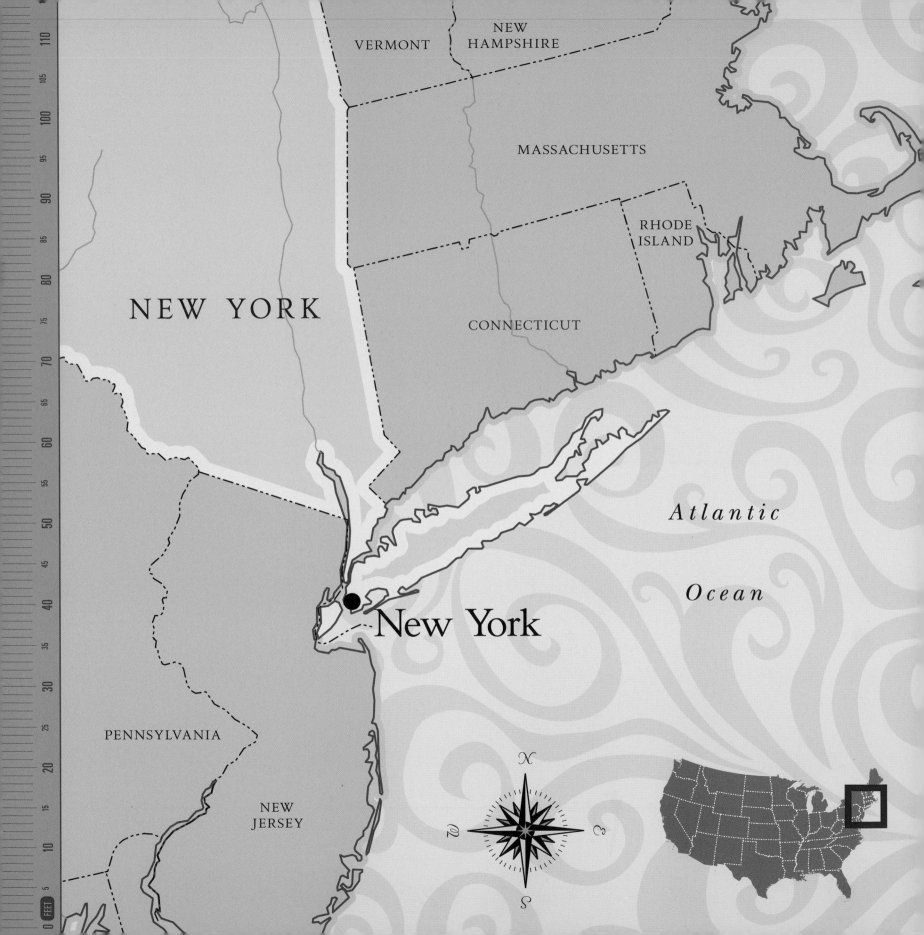

NEW YORK

VERMONT

NEW HAMPSHIRE

MASSACHUSETTS

RHODE ISLAND

CONNECTICUT

Atlantic

Ocean

New York

PENNSYLVANIA

NEW JERSEY

N

W

E

S

The Empire State Building is a building called a skyscraper. It is in New York City. It is so tall that it looks like it can touch the sky!

The Empire State Building is New York's tallest skyscraper

6

The state of New York is called "The Empire State." That is where the name of the building came from. A man named William Lamb designed the Empire State Building. It was built to hold lots of offices.

The Flatiron and Woolworth buildings were early New York City skyscrapers.

Skyscraper builders often had to work at dangerous heights

8

In 1930, about 3,000 workers started building the Empire State Building. They worked every single day. It took 1 year and 45 days to finish the 102-story building. It was made out of hard rocks called limestone and granite.

William Lamb based his design for the building on a pencil

The Empire State Building is 1,472 feet (449 m) tall today.

The Empire State Building opened on May 1, 1931. People celebrated by climbing all 1,860 steps to get to the top. Many people liked how pretty the building was. They thought it was a work of art.

In 1983, an inflatable King Kong was put on top of the Empire State Building.

The first movie to star the ape King Kong was made in 1933

The Empire State Building was the tallest building in the world for 40 years. Today, it is the tallest building in New York City. Lots of people have seen the building in movies. In the movie *King Kong*, a giant ape climbs on top of the building.

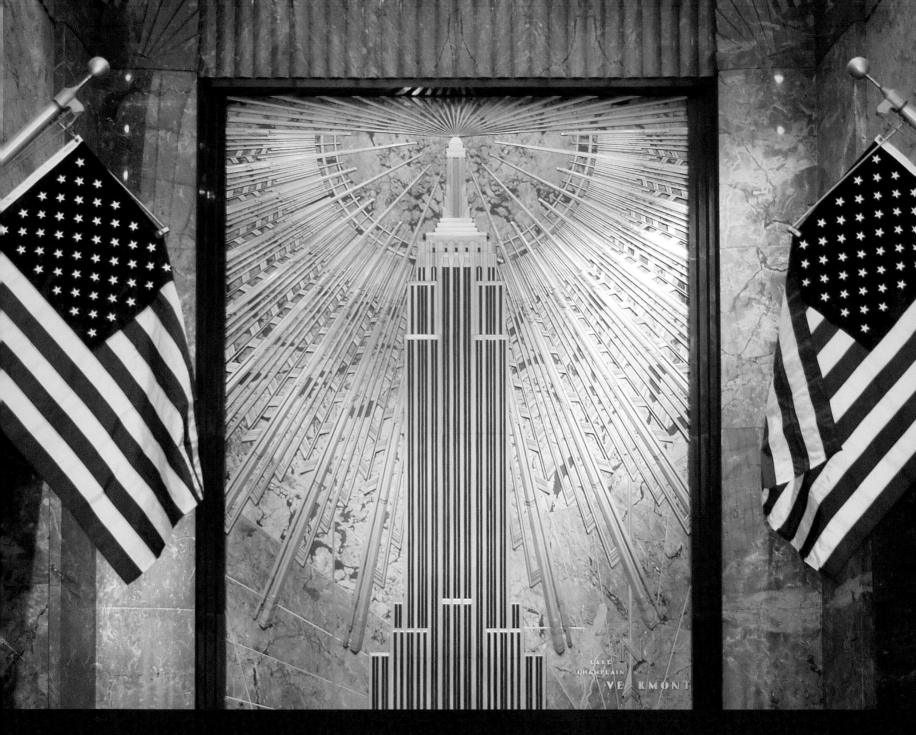

The first-floor lobby welcomes visitors to the building

The Empire State Building is taller than the Eiffel Tower and the Great Pyramid put together!

People love working in or visiting the Empire State Building. The big building is a **symbol** of how great things are possible in America.

From the decks, visitors can see across New York City

16

More than 3.5 million people tour the Empire State Building every year. They walk up the stairs or take an elevator to get to the **observation decks**. The decks are outside the building on the 86th and 102nd floors. People can see a long way from there.

The Empire State Building towers over all others around it

18

The top of the Empire State Building gets struck by lightning about 100 times per year!

New York has cold winters and hot summers. But the observation decks are open every day. Lots of people like to visit New York in the fall. It is cooler then.

The Empire State Building is lit up in different colors for holidays and special events.

22

23

GLOSSARY

designed—*drew up plans for*

inflatable—*something that can be blown up with air*

observation decks—*areas high up on the outsides of buildings where people can go to see the views*

offices—*rooms where work is done as part of a business*

symbol—*a thing that stands for something else*

READ MORE ABOUT IT

Hopkinson, Deborah. *Sky Boys: How They Built the Empire State Building*. New York: Random House, 2006.

Mann, Elizabeth. *The Empire State Building: When New York Reached for the Skies*. New York: Mikaya Press, 2003.

24

INDEX